Teddywood
Bear Village and Fairy Glen

A Fun Guide to
Leadhills History

Lee Stewart Gilmore

ISBN: 10 1514237768
ISBN-13: 978-1514237762

To Ruby & Annie

DEDICATION

This book is dedicated to all the past inhabitants of Leadhills who left us
with such a wealth of history and achievement.

I hope I am doing you proud and helping to keep your legacy alive.

with Love
Auntie Kee &
chester
xx.

CONTENTS

Acknowledgments   i

1   Introduction   Pg 5

2   Grampa Sam   Pg 7

3   Doc Martin   Pg 9

4   Ebearnezer Hall   Pg 11

5   Mr Ramsay   Pg 13

6   Curfew Bell   Pg 15

7   Mr Symington   Pg 17

8   Mr Stirling   Pg 19

9   Mr Taylor   Pg 21

10   Mrs Stewart   Pg 22

11   Hillbilly Sarah   Pg 23

12   Fairyland   Pg 24

ACKNOWLEDGMENTS

Thank you to everyone who donated items used in the building of Teddywood and to the friends and neighbours who lent me tools and helped carry houses and heavy supplies up into the Bear Village.

Thank you to all my customers at Bear-ly Reminiscent for their support and their donations

TEDDYWOOD
BEAR VILLAGE

LEADHILLS

Teddywood and Fairyland

Leadhills has always been referred to as 'remote', and I expect in the 1700's and 1800's, remote would have been an understatement. We have today, in the 21st century, caught up with the times. We are 7 miles from the M74 at Abington on the B797. I tell you this, because if you use your SatNav, you may end up in Biggar which is 20 miles in the opposite direction. Well, some things haven't quite caught up with us.

Leadhills in the 18th and 19th centuries produced remarkable people. They were well educated and very self sufficient and way ahead of their time in respect of other mining communities in the country. The schoolmasters were available to both miners and their children and classes were held for both. A university education was attainable for many.

Pedlars visited the village, travelling from Edinburgh and as well as carrying products that weren't available in the village, would also uplift goods from the village to be sold in Edinburgh.

Leadhills was known as a Jacobite area and was also involved in the Covenanters movement, so they weren't afraid to speak their minds or stand by their beliefs. I think we are still like that today, although we haven't been known to hide anyone fleeing the authorities for quite some time.

Teddywood Bear Village is part of Bear-ly Reminiscent, the home of the famous Leadhills Mining Bears. Each of the bear characters has his own house in the village along with a schoolhouse, church and a Fairy Glen. A walk through the village will give you an insight into Leadhills History and the amazing characters that lived here.

The Teddywood Bear Village is built on the hillside so paths may be slightly uneven and young children should be supervised. The nearest hospital is 40 miles away.

Enjoy your visit to Scotland's Highest Bear Village and as they say here.......HASTE YE BACK.

Glengonnar Mine was situated on the left-hand side of the road as you head from Leadhills over to Wanlockhead and the ruins are clearly visible today. The mine closed in the 1930's

2. GRAMPA SAM

Although Grampa Sam is not strictly part of Leadhills history he is still much a part of village life. Grampa Sam sits outside the Bear Shop each day in his basket chair with his little dog Jacob. As part of the Leadhills Mining Bear Company, Grampa Sam is now retired and is responsible for educating the younger bears on the village's past. He is the village storyteller and his house is the first on your tour of Teddywood.

JAMES MARTIN

DOC MARTIN THE BEAR

3. DOC MARTIN

James Martin 1790 – 1875. James Martin graduated from the Royal College of Surgeons in Edinburgh when he was 21. He joined the Military and became Wellington's direct surgeon during the Napoleonic Wars. For his last year of military service he was transferred to the West Indies and missed the Battle of Waterloo by a matter of months. He met his wife, a British citizen, who was born in Jamaica and returned with her as a new bride to Leadhills. The poor girl must have been horrified after living in the West Indian climate, but they remained in Leadhills and raised their family. They had seven children in total. On his return from the West Indies, James qualified at Edinburgh University as a General Practitioner and became the doctor in Leadhills. They lived on East Row in the village, now part of Main St. and he later became Bailiff for Hopetoun Estates.

James died in Edinburgh at the age of 85 and is buried in Leadhills Cemetery.

EBENEZER HALL

4. EBEARNEZER HALL
(EBENEZER HALL)

The Ebenezer Hall was built in 1905 as a Plymouth Brethren Meeting Hall and was the old Leadhills Free Church. Leadhills had 3 churches. One was at the end of Ramsay Road where it meets Gowanbank, the Lowther Parish Church on Main Street and the Ebenezer Hall which today has been transformed into luxury holiday accommodation. The Ebearnezer Hall is the Bears' church.

ALLAN RAMSAY

MR RAMSAY THE BEAR

5. MR RAMSAY

Allan Ramsay (1686 – 1758)

Allan Ramsay was the son of John Ramsay, superintendent of Lord Hopetoun's mine. He established himself as a wig-maker in Edinburgh's High Street before becoming one of Scotland's most famous poets. He later moved to another shop in the Luckenbooths where he opened a circulating library, the first in Scotland, and extended his business as a bookseller. He retired in 1755 to his house on the slope of the Castle Rock, still known as Ramsay Lodge. He is buried at Greyfriars Churchyard, Edinburgh.
His eldest son was Allan Ramsay, the portrait painter.

The Curfew Bell and Mr Aitchison the Bear

6. THE CURFEW BELL

The Curfew Bell was built in 1770 in honour of James Stirling, the mine manager. It rang the changes in the shifts at the mine; it rang for the school and was also used in the event of a mine accident.

These days the bell is only rung to bring in the New Year, by the oldest member of the oldest family, a duty currently held by Mr Aitchison.

William Symington and Mr Symington the Bear

7. MR SYMINGTON

William Symington, (1764-1831).

William Symington, born in Leadhills, was a mining engineer at the mine in Wanlockhead. His claim to fame however, was for inventing the world's first steamship. Initial trials were held at Dalswinton Loch in 1788. Lord Dundas gave Symington his support for the building of a second boat which was named after one of his daughter's, and so the 'Charlotte Dundas' was born and sailed in 1803. There is an obelisk monument to Symington in the village overlooking the house where he was born and situated in front of the graveyard.

There are no known portraits of James Stirling, but here's one of his house and we do know what he looks like as a bear.
Mr Strling the Bear

8. MR STIRLING

James Stirling (1692-1770). Mr Stirling was our most notable mine manager. He studied at Oxford and became a renowned mathematician with a shrewd business sense. Unfortunately for him, his family connection to the Jacobite cause prevented him having a career in London and on returning to Scotland he joined the Scots Mining Company as Manager of the mine in Leadhills. He vastly improved the living and working conditions of the miners and he more than tripled the productivity of the mine. William Adam, the famous architect was commissioned to build a house for Mr Stirling and as he normally built stately homes, the house in Leadhills is a large mansion house, complete with servants' quarters and a stable block. The actual Scots Mining Company house is currently painted white but I didn't think he would mind if his bear house was pink.

There are no portraits of John Taylor so
here is Mr Taylor the Bear

9. MR TAYLOR

John Taylor (1633-1770) was born in Alston Moor in Cumberland but spent the majority of his working life in the lead mines in Scotland and finally coming to Leadhills in 1733 and worked as a miner until 1752, having spent upwards of a century in unceasing work. John Taylor witnessed the total eclipse in 1652 as a young lad working in the mine.

He is buried in our graveyard and his headstone clearly states, 'Here lies John Taylor who died in his 137th year'.

His description is as follows: He was a thin spare man, about 5ft 8ins in height, black haired, ruddy faced, and long visaged – with a healthy appetite. He walked the hills until he was almost 130 years old. When he was 120 years, he did get lost in a sudden snow storm and thought his time had come. He was found on the hillside and brought back to the village. The following day he returned to the hillside to recover his fishing pole that he had left stuck in the snow.

10. MRS STEWART

Although strictly speaking Mrs Stewart isn't part of Leadhills history, as far as the bears are concerned, she is the entrepreneur of wife bears. Extremely good at making jam, she opened a little Jam Factory on the hillside. She employs the Hillbillies.

11. HILLBILLY SARAH

One of the Hillbilly clan that live high on the hillside. The Hillbillies are too lazy to work in the mine and are the poachers in the area. In the winter they work for Mrs Stewart in the Jam Factory.

Hillbilly Sarah gathers the berries and herbs for making the jam and unlike the rest of her clan, she works all year at the Jam Factory.

12. FAIRYLAND

It wouldn't be a Scottish village without some fairies running around. Contrary to popular belief, not all Scottish fairies were sweet little creatures. We had our fair share of fairy legends, where they stole children, and adults wandering at night alone disappeared never to return. Worse than most were the Kelpies. They took the form of beautiful horses generally near water. People were so enthralled with the amazing horses they climbed onto their back, at which point the Kelpie charged into the sea with their captive. But of course Teddywood has no such fairies. We have flower fairies and tooth fairies. The Tooth Fairy houses are distinct in that the house changes when a child has toothache and that's how the Tooth Fairy knows to come and pick up a tooth. It's an education visiting Teddywood.

24

I HOPE YOU HAVE ENJOYED YOUR VISIT TO TEDDYWOOD AND THAT YOU WILL RETURN. THERE ARE A FEW MORE HOUSES TO BE ADDED AND HOPEFULLY MORE BENCHES AND TABLES. IT HAS BEEN A PLEASURE MEETING YOU.

LEE STEWART GILMORE
AND
CHESTER THE 'MAD' CAVALIER XX

bear-lyreminiscent.com
or find us on Facebook

If you have the time you may wish to leave a review on tripadvisor.

Don't forget to visit our shop.

18108963R00019

Printed in Great Britain
by Amazon